Sailing West

Sailing West
Carol Coffee Reposa

ISBN: 978-1-942956-44-0

Editor: Katie Odom

Lamar University Literary Press
Beaumont, TX

To my students, who for 42 years showed me the way, with special thanks to friend and guru Tom Murphy.

Recent Poetry from Lamar University Literary Press

Lisa Adams, *Xuai*
Walter Bargen, *My Other Mother's Red Mercedes*
Jerry Bradley, *Collapsing into Possibility*
Mark Busby, *Through Our Times*
Julie Chappell, *Mad Habits of a Life*
Stan Crawford, *Resisting Gravity*
Glover Davis, *My Cap of Darkness*
William Virgil Davis, *The Bones Poems*
Jeffrey DeLotto, *Voices Writ in Sand*
Chris Ellery, *Elder Tree*
Dede Fox, *On Wings of Silence*
Alan Gann, *That's Entertainment*
Larry Griffin, *Cedar Plums*
Michelle Hartman, *Irony and Irrelevance*
Katherine Hoerth, *Goddess Wears Cowboy Boots*
Michael Jennings, *Crossings: A Record of Travel*
Gretchen Johnson, *A Trip Through Downer, Minnesota*
Betsy Joseph, *Only So Many Autumns*
Ulf Kirchdorfer, *Chewing Green Leaves*
Jim McGarrah, *A Balancing Act*
J. Pittman McGehee, *Nod of Knowing*
Laurence Musgrove, *Bluebonnet Sutras*
Benjamin Myers, *Black Sunday*
Janice Northerns, *Some Electric Hum*
Godspower Oboido, *Wandering Feet on Pebbled Shores*
Carol Coffee Reposa, *Underground Musicians*
Jan Seale, *Particulars*
Steven Schroeder, *the moon, not the finger, pointing*
Glen Sorestad, *Hazards of Eden*
Vincent Spina, *The Sumptuous Hills of Gulfport*
W.K. Stratton, *Betrayal Creek*
Wally Swist, *Invocation*
Ken Waldman, *Sports Page*
Loretta Diane Walker, *Ode to My Mother's Voice*
Dan Williams, *Past Purgatory, a Distant Paradise*
Jonas Zdanys, *The Angled Road*

For information on these and other Lamar University Literary
Press books go to www.Lamar.edu/literarypress

Acknowledgements

The author acknowledges with gratitude the following journals and anthologies in which some of these poems first appeared:

Amarillo Bay, Blue Hole, C.20. An International Journal, CCTE Studies, CEA SCOL, Cinco de VIA, Dragon Poet Review, easing the edges, a collection of everyday miracles, English in Texas, The Enigmatist, Fire to Light Our Tongues, The Great American Wise-Ass Poetry Anthology, Illya's Honey, Langdon Review of the Arts (2018, 2020), The Larger Geometry. Poems for Peace, New Texas, Prompts and Pathways, Pushing the Envelope: Epistolary Poems, Red River Review, RiverSedge, The San Antonio Express-News, SA 24. Two Dozen Songs from Now, Switchgrass Review, Tejascovido, Tex!, The Texas Observer, Texas Poetry Ballots, Texas Poetry Calendar (2004, 2005, 2014, 2021), Texas Weather, Through Layered Limestone, Voices de la Luna, and *Writing Texas 2020.*

CONTENTS

Texas, Our Texas?

Almost Gods

Crossing Over

Texas, Our Texas?

Homage to the Valley Palms

They sway
Along the Interstate
In their endless rumba,
Ten thousand showgirls
In outrageous hats,
Those bobbing green plumes.

At the coast they high-kick
In leggy legions to the beat
Of waves, toddlers shrieking
And dogs barking rapturously
In salt spray, wind surfers
And kites above them,
Teens showing off bikinis.

Inland, they stage production numbers
Day and night, chorus lines
Everywhere, at hospitals
And banks, strip centers
And parking lots,
Irrigation ditches and fields.
They see it all:

Dizzy spinach, sugarcane
And bouncing cabbages,
Grapefruit glowing in their trees,
Drug-sniffing dogs at the border,
A deal going down
In an alley,
First Communions and Last Rites.

North of Edinburg
The show winds down. At Encino
I think they've taken
Their last bow, but in Alice
One straggler throws me
A boa. I make a one-hand catch.

A Galveston Palimpsest

I'm back on the balcony. Here
Time blurs into an everlasting present,
The Gulf a great gray heart
Pulsing through everything, ebb and flow,
Point and counterpoint.
Seagulls forever spiral
Through steamy afternoons,
Their wings forever stretched
Into sky, a copper sun
Forever floating
Over a line of palms.

The CEO of something
Sips a mojito, drops
His *Wall Street Journal* in the spa,
Watches toddlers in pink floaties
At the shallow end
Of the pool
While my aunt, BOI,
Hosts a cookout on Stewart Beach.

My first love and I savor
Coney Islands and lemonade
At the end of a pier in 1965,
Salt spray in our hair, sand
Crusting our fingers as waves break
Over the jetty and a pair of dolphins
Arch ecstatic over the bay
In their perfect sleek parabolas.

It's 1922. My grandparents prepare
To take the waters
In their heavy bathing garb.
Mom, age four, poses before
The newly completed Seawall.
Her younger brother, worried, gazes
At the Gulf, a faithful servant
In the background.

Now it's World War I. A heedless uncle
Swims out too far, vanishes
In a riptide, remains
Never found. Grandmother loses
Three cousins in the Great Storm of 1900,
All swept into that counterclockwise apocalypse,
Roaring labyrinth, those crashing walls
Of sea. The letter arrives four weeks late.

Today, bare-chested cyclists
Pedal along the Strand. Beyond them
Tourists gather shells
And beachcombers work metal detectors.
Along the shoreline, someone's written
"Cody Loves Nicole" in letters four feet high,
Big enough for the sun, moon, and every star
To see until the tide
Rolls in
Rolls out
Forever.

Port Bolivar after Hurricane Ike

I've come to see her
One more time,
This wrinkled diva
With a giant heart.
I want to hear it beat,
To touch that face
That shines for miles.

Generous and sloppy,
She slings iridescent baubles
Everywhere she goes, a parade queen
Throwing candy to the throngs.
She conjures ribs in sand, scatters
Conch shells east and west,
Festoons the world in kelp.

Sometimes she turns moody,
Rages, spits out torrents
Shreds her belongings,
Tears things
To splinters,
Even feeds
On her young.

But then as suddenly
She stops,
Resumes her usual largesse
Smiles her glittering smile
And rubs
The world's back
Until it sleeps.

Sandfest, Port "A"

For a weekend, they come back to life:
Knights and mermaids,
Gnomes, unicorns and demons.
Temporary castles
Rise on the beach,
Their crenellations shaped
By sunburned men and women
Working against a clock.
Their gritty hands shave ramparts smooth as marble,
Cut the dragon's scales in perfect overlap
Leaving him to guard
The iridescent blobs of jellyfish
With snowbirds watching everything.

Out in the Gulf
Tankers lumber through the swells
And shrimp boats spread their nets,
A fawning entourage of seagulls
In their wake
Fighting wave wars
With dive-bombing pelicans
While the sea rolls in
And battlements take shape
Beneath the hands
Of magicians
In a dead heat
With the tide.

Lighthouse, Port Isabel

We enter
A chrysalis
Of peeling plaster,
Plod up the spiral staircase,
Pant toward sea and sky.

Suddenly I'm in
A Christmas Carol, watching the Ghost
Of Christmas Past drag Scrooge
To an unwilling glimpse
Of keepers joining hands

During a storm,
Kindness in a gale
While rogue waves crash
Against the tower,
Blur the flashing lamp.

We reach the top,
Take in a breathless Gulf
Tranquil at the moment
Despite tempests come and gone,
Battles fought.

Ships were lost here, many drowned,
But still I think this beacon
Is perfection, sending out
Its swirling slice of light
Forever
Into dark.

Cedar Fever

The effects: twelve sneezes over coffee
Trash cans stuffed
With sodden Kleenex, wads of tears
Hot streams
Trickling down the cheeks,
Itching in the throat
That speaking doesn't scratch.

The cause: green flames
Shooting up brown hillsides
In the worst of January,
Spiked emeralds erupting
From the miles
And miles
Of winter.

Smoldering by farm-to-market roads
They jump blacktops everywhere,
A blaze
That speaks a hundred pungent tongues
And climbs
Into gray skies
To heat the afternoon.

Travis Park, 2016

Slow cadences of rain
Coat everything today.
Drops sift through oaks, bead up
The bronze Confederate's face,
Roll down his neck. Acorns fall
To the walkway
In percussive plops,
Split around his feet.

Above, fat pigeons posture
On the Rebel's broad-brimmed hat.
He poses like the archetypal soldier,
One granite hand raised constantly
Toward something while the other
Grips his Sharps. I read
"Lest We Forget" in high relief
Below a laurel wreath.

Leftover cannon guard
Each corner of the space, their polished
Five-inch bores pointed out into the city
In frozen pantomime,
A cryptic vigil against an undetermined foe
While cars and trucks, children and tourists
Circle the hero in their dusty pageant,
Slowly choking his gray heart.

Homeless in Waco

They gather
Underneath the Interstate,
Circle paltry fires

To form a ragged coda
In the march of shrines and domes,
White spires

Puncturing the January sky,
Mansions stating themes
In brick and stone

Fluted colonnades
And Doric capitals,
Shutters closing off

The scrawny descants
Rising in the streets
Beneath a heaven of cement

Withered voices
Underneath the bridge
Drowned in the vamp

Of wrought iron fences,
Intercoms and cell phones
Guards who think they do not hear.

Fable for the Red Dynasties

The opulent ladies' room
Was daunting, a fussy rhapsody
In lace and polished brass.
Almost afraid to touch
The embroidered towelettes
I suddenly remembered college years long gone,
Those endless trips to Austin,
Late-night stops in one-horse towns.

Once, in one of them, I sought
The bathroom, found a peeling door.
Inside, a light bulb swayed
Like something out of *Psycho*.
Through its murky light I saw
A grimy toilet, seat up, flanking
A cracked urinal, the washstand buried
Beneath a palimpsest of scum.

By the crusted spigots
Was a bowl of shaving soap,
Its stiff brush waiting
For a beard or legs or underarms.
On the wall one dispenser
Offered cheap cologne; another, condoms.
Over the second was a sign: "For hygienic
Purposes only. Any other use against the law,"

Hypocrisy beneath an overlay
Of public service, out of place
In the brawling Sixties,
Time of burning flags and bras
Vietnam and riots
Freedom rides and sit-ins,
Not so different from today:

Children lost in the name
Of family values, millions
Left behind, women shrunk
To genital appliances, epoch of double-think

Born again with water-boarding canonized,
Land dark under a promise
Of clear skies, a nation gasping,
Staggering
Beneath the yoke
Of freedom.

The CBP Official Writes a Sonnet for Reporters at the Detention Facility in Clint, Texas

Please rest assured, we have no crisis here.
It's true we're short on toothpaste, diapers, soap
And workers sometimes find it hard to cope
With all that crying in the cells, their fear
Of those who drink from toilets, or the tear
That streaks a toddler's dirty face, no hope
In her dark eyes. But we've no time to mope
About such things, for more invaders clear
Our borders in another wave each day,
More caravans. They could do worse. Our beds
Of concrete beat the places where they slept
Before, in shit-hole countries where they kept
No running water in their filthy sheds.
No baths? So what? That's all I've got to say.

Pantoum for Mineral Wells

Beneath the crumbling concrete, peeling walls,
Old times rise up from under rust and rock--
Those endless parties, concerts, lavish balls—
They're all freeze-framed today. There is no clock.

Old times rise up from under rust and rock.
Ghosts gaze out on their vacant town, nonplussed.
They're all freeze-framed today. There is no clock,
Just silence on the haunted streets, and dust.

Ghosts gaze out on their vacant town, nonplussed,
To see the dingy burger joints and stands.
Just silence on the haunted streets, and dust
Before those spectral faces, empty hands.

To see those dingy burger joints and stands,
"For Sale" signs everywhere, and shuttered stores.
Before those spectral faces, empty hands,
The past pours out through windows, bolted doors.

"For Sale" signs everywhere, and shuttered stores
That grand hotel, the Baker, rises still.
The past pours out through windows, bolted doors.
A ragged sentinel atop a hill,

That grand hotel, the Baker, rises still.
Hallucination in red brick, it stays,
A ragged sentinel atop a hill
Outlasting ice storms, hail storms, searing days

Hallucination in red brick, it stays,
An avatar beneath a hard blue sky
Outlasting ice storms, hail storms, searing days
Reminder of what's lost, a silent sigh.

Those endless parties, concerts, lavish balls
Unfold in empty rooms and phantom space
Beneath the crumbling concrete, peeling walls,
Vast fossil of a vanished time and place.

Sunflowers

Sprouting near fences
Rooting by dumpsters
Inching through cracks
In the sidewalk
Erupting between beer cans
In alleys,
They sprawl
Across Texas
May to November.

Oblivious
To heat or drought,
They send out leaves
In prodigal legions,
Their great green hearts
Beating everywhere
Beneath a blue steel sky,
Finally enfolding us all
In gold.

Driving to San Angelo

Once I leave the Interstate,
Road signs spell out high hopes
And whimsy. At Volkmann Draw
I whip out a giant sketchbook.
Spoon Draw makes me hungry
And I wolf down miles of mesquite,
Hear 10,000 croaks
At Frog Pond Creek.
I steer clear of Ditch Walk
But Gentry Creek refines me and in London
I almost hear Big Ben. Paradise awaits
In Eden, treasure in Eldorado.
Veribest rolls out the perfect blacktop,
Making Ripple Road smoother than still wine.

But whatever road I take,
For the last 30 miles all signs point
To cotton bolls bouncing
On barbed wire and fence posts
Under an electric blue sky
That charges everything,
A hardscrabble symphony of wind
That moves through my skin,
Fills veins with likable grit
And makes me want to jump
From the car, wave my arms,
Whirl to a windmill's creaky song
Like a liberated scarecrow
With nothing to do but dance.

Interlude

We fill the August night
Forever
Swinging, swinging
On the porch,
Swaying to the white noise
Of the moon
While she glides
Between telephone wires
Through trees
In and out of clouds
All night,
Floating in her tranquil sea
Or balancing on stars,
The longest ballet ever
While we are
Swinging, swinging
On the porch,
Fireflies dancing
In the dark
A minor fireworks show
In oaks and ivy
Swinging, swinging
On the porch.

Weekend at Lake Travis

At sunrise
There is nothing
But one lazy sail on the lake

The whirring of a fan,
Sharp scent of cedars
When the wind lifts

In a hundred shades of green.
Later on, we amble through the brush,
Our black Labs nuzzling everything

And startling families of deer,
Their hooves clattering to silence
On white limestone.

That night
It's barbeque and beer,
Old jokes and family stories,

Voices drifting out over the water,
Caught up in the blue wake
Of a passing outboard

As it rumbles home toward the marina
And its wavy line of lights
Beneath a swirl of shooting stars.

Sunday Houses, Fredericksburg

I know now
Why the Germans built them,
Farmers giving up their days of rest
For years
To lay up limestone, plane red oaks,
Bumping through sweaty mornings
On a buckboard
Just to sit out on the porch
And watch light drift
Through scraggly pines.

Yearning for the Rhine
And lush green hills,
They needed one day's leave
From sun and toil,
One vacant space in the week
So they could sit
In sparsely furnished rooms
And talk of almost nothing
With the neighbors, take in nightfall,
Contemplate the flames
In smoky lamps.

Chronic exiles,
They arranged their lives
In tight compartments,
Some cluttered
With others almost bare,
Thought swinging
Like a rough-hewn pendulum
From one chamber to the next and back
In lurching rhythms,
Almost like a dance.

Dawn in El Paso

Above the cinderblocks
Pocked sidewalks
Beer and Pepsi cans
Lined up along the streets
Like soldiers,

Light slides down
The Franklins
In a ragged progress,
Drops sun
In charcoal pockets

And purple clefts,
Colors shifting
On the mountain face
Like crumpled taffeta
As early morning

Ripples down slopes
And peels the night
From patient stones
In acts
Of random grace.

Migration of the Butterflies

They shimmer, splash
Through autumn afternoons,
Confetti in unlikely places
Celebrating traffic, trees and streets.

Waltzing by the thousands
Through their giant ballroom,
Lacewings, morphos, monarchs, julias
Lock in oblivious embrace

Whirl around each other
Breathless in gold,
Russet, amber, blue.
They dance into everything,

Giddy children spinning
While they end
A verse
Of "London Bridge"

Or catch
The wildest ride
In the amusement park
Like skaters

Who have worked the ice
Too long, their leaps too high,
Speed
About to hurl them

Past the old, familiar ring
North
South
Beyond.

In the Permian Basin

Even in October
Light sweeps into everything:
Pale, determined
Rolling into concrete
Undersides of mesquite leaves
Spikes of cactus
Spaces under doors.

Sunshine flattens
Even thoughts
Of height
While empty skies
Bend buildings into dots,
Willows into tumbleweeds
Fences into twigs.

The wind clears everything.
A vagrant
Never stopping
Anywhere too long,
His boots
Leave nothing
On the Interstate.

His hat forever blows
Into vermilion sunsets
When he whips out
His harmonica
To orchestrate the dark.
And all night long
Trees dance.

Short Ode to the West Texas Wind

She comes out of nowhere,
A madcap fighter pilot
Strafing the staked plains
On a whim,
Dame Fortune
Briefly leaving her wheel.

She's that slap
In the face, undeserved,
That kick in the rear
The car door
Slamming into your hand.
She's the salesman
Who shoves his foot
Through the door
And won't take no
For an answer.
She's the one-liner
That stops conversation,
A flash-poetry mob
Suddenly materializing
In the mall,
A breaking story interrupting
The nightly news,
That midnight ring tone
Shattering sleep.

But before she whirls away
To spin her wheel again
She backhands dust and damp,
Polishes the sun's gold face
And scours the heavens
Until they shine.

October in South Texas

It's here again,
That flame-throwing time
When trees hurl sparks and embers
Down the streets,
Onto rooftops
Across windows.

Even in this library
Reds, ochres, golds
Are seeping
Through pallid walls
And blazing
Along the dusty stacks,

Coating all the books
And faded posters
Even the threadbare rug
With stored-up color
And light,
Enough to last for months.

In San Pedro Springs Park

Ninety yards from traffic
And a killer intersection
Thick with fumes and dour facades
The mystery erupts,
An emerald sphinx
Surrounded by winter brown

And 12,000 years of community,
Old oaks bearing still the imprint of Payayas
And Franciscans, the first
Of the two Alamos,
Canary Islanders and Buffalo Soldiers, later on
The homeless briefly coming home.

The locked tower
Looks unlikely here,
Something from Arthurian romance
The Green Knight waiting
For Sir Gawain
With a password or a trial.

Water hisses like a reclusive snake
Coiled somewhere in its limestone walls,
Whispering its riddle hours on end
Behind the ferns that curl
Through moss in dark green tufts
Of otherworldly hair.

Ice water drips
Down the fronds, down the monolith
Questioning forever all who pass
In a language lost
As we move away
Toward the brick-and-mortar world beyond.

In Late November

for Ruth

The music has begun,
And leaves on my red oak
Start to drift away
In their slow sleepy waltz
But already
Frost-hard roots
Are tuning up
For an April allegro
In the key
Of neon green.

San Antonio Blizzard, 1985

She blew in one afternoon,
A witch
Who wrapped the world
In stiff white sheets
That snapped into a thousand splinters
With each step.

Later, she made sunset disappear
And filled heaven
With a languid vast ballet,
Dancers whirling slowly
On and off the stage
All night.

In the morning
She bleached streets and trees,
Drew light
Into a silence of bare branches,
Hardened sun
Along the eaves.

Then she noticed her reflection
In the soft bewildered gaze of animals,
Watched the flutter of cold wings
As sparrows struggled oak to oak
Before she turned toward home,
Leaving the dazzled land.

Arctic Ice Storm, San Antonio

Ice sweeps across the city
In a wave. The rave
Goes on for days and nights,
Millions hungry for the limelight,
Jostling to be seen. Wearing nothing
But rhinestones and lame,
They leave a trail
Of sequins on the prickly pears
And mesquites,
Climb on palms and rooftops,
Won't let us look
At anything else.

Then one morning, they tire
Of fame. Yearning suddenly
For a getaway, perhaps
Some island in the tropics,
The weary glitterati
Start to yawn and slump.
Finally they sleep,
Collapsing on the streets
In noisy heaps
Leaving nothing
But a shining pool
Of memory.

Moonrise, San Antonio

She stops my breath
During rush hour, a full moon
Floating across a clear December sky,
Cleopatra on her barge.

Briefly visiting royalty,
She is the queen
Of everything, rising
Over rooftops and billboards,
Interstates and the Alamo
Far-flung burbs and inner-city high rises,
San Fernando
And the Riverwalk.

She moves to music
We can't hear, maybe
A cosmic barcarole.
I strain my ears
To catch the melody,
Almost drive off the road
Oblivious to bills and bureaucracy,
Debts and deadlines

While she shelters
Us all
In the warm folds
Of her ivory velvet robe.

Almost Gods

Assyrian Pitcher

Mounted on an off-white pedestal
Behind thick glass,
Illuminated by a single shaft
Of light

The vessel looks
Like nothing
Made to pour scarce water
On a thirsty tongue.

I can not picture
Wine
Or even nectar
Flowing from its spout.

Unreally green,
A shade beyond naming
Caught in a blank space
Somewhere in the spectrum,

Its tint conjures oceans
No one ever saw,
Their depths rich with embryonic life,
Their colors cresting somewhere

On a high primordial wave
Thick with salt and light
When salt and light were holy,
Almost gods.

Sculpture of Ariadne, Sleeping

She reclines against an outcrop
On the island of Naxos, lost
To everything except her dreams.
At her side a bird of prey
Attacks a lizard. Her glowing arms
Encircle her head, the drape
Falling from her breast.

She does not yet know
That Theseus
Has left her there,
Fresh from his triumph
In battle with the Minotaur
To seek another port,
Perhaps another woman.

When she wakes, will she rail
At his ingratitude,
Shake her luminous fists
At his memory
After she gave him the thread
That led him from the Labyrinth,
Gave him the years to come?

Will she take up life
In this abandoned place, watch over
Its rough animals and scratch out
Her days on white stones? Will she scan
The seas for wayward ships or simply wait
For the gods to intervene? Can she put
Those wine-dark nights behind her?

For now she sleeps
In perfect marble silence,
Tranquil
In her thoughts
Of everything
She doesn't know
She's lost.

Imperial Roman Art Show

I walk through rooms
Of marble busts
Some still ivory
Despite the twenty centuries,
Others faintly gold
Like antique lace.

Caligula is streaked with brown,
Dun flecks in his rounded eyes
Most of the faces missing noses
Or an ear
And even then
They look serene

As if they spent their time
At luncheons or the country club
Beyond the reach of war,
Disease or famine
Everything symmetrical
At home

Women weaving days
Into tranquil shapes,
The dog in dutiful attendance
While they reverenced their household gods,
Designing and inscribing tombs—
"Claudia made this..."

They lived oblivious to blood, to flame,
Even the lava soon to bury them
While they had sex
On a fine Carrara couch
Or took their baths,
A bunch of grapes in either hand.

Envelope and Envelop: A Brief History

His two profiles
Facing opposite directions,
Janus must have wrought
These uneasy twins
While he was guarding
His gates and doorways,
Watching what came through
Or went out: mists wreathing
Barren hills, softening their crags
And filling their depths,
Or rain sheathing the desert
In a healing sheet of gray.
Maybe he saw a herald triumphant
Unroll his scroll
To proclaim victory afar,
Or another messenger leap
From his lathered horse to announce a plague
In the East, enfolding the city in fear.

In later times
He might have noticed
The mailman delivering
Thin windowed envelopes,
Their sickly yellow
Containing words
That wrapped the world in tears
Like acid rain or Oklahoma dust,
But sometimes
The courier might have brought
Creamy containers
Of parties, weddings, births
Perhaps an award
Enveloping all
In warmth
Holding off the cold, the dark
Like a down comforter
On a night of January sleet.

Elizabeth I on the Knighting of Drake

I laughed and told him I would take his head
That day he knelt before me on the deck
Of his worn ship, his hands and face still flecked
With gold he tore from the unwilling bed
Of Spain, who burns for upstart blood. Instead,
I supped with him before I touched his neck
To make him blameless. Others try to check
Him. Burleigh spurns his gifts, to prudence wed.
But I will shroud those peers who scorn Drake's crest.
I'll wear the emerald crown that he entailed.
For in his gaze I see my scepter curled,
Jeweled sails that magnified this island, pressed
Magellan to his wake, in waves that scaled
New stars and made of my small shores, the world.

Viewing a Spanish Art Exhibit

Light streams
Across El Greco's Christ,
His angular face
And slightly twisted neck, beyond
The swaggering bullfighters
Posing with their cigars,
Those rosy-cheeked infantas
In their gold brocade,
Those generals
With the fringed epaulettes.

Already his thoughts turn
Toward heaven. The Savior sees
Past the sunbaked hills of Toledo
Rising in rich russet
From the rocks,
The cloistered green
Of a walled garden,
A mother about to take the waters
While her playful children
Splash through light
In their diaphanous dresses,
Those saccharine cherubs
Even the assorted Annunciations
And Crucifixions.

Beyond the lace and ruffles,
Outside the museum's stately walls
He contemplates the youth
Lying dead in the street, those deserts
Of crumbling brick, venom in the air.
The edges of his halo dissolve
Under an indifferent sky
As his luminous eyes
Encompass everything,
And Calvary continues.

Meditation on a Late van Gogh

Somewhere in Holland
Tulips sprawl
Across a sodden field
In rows of orange, yellow, red
Before a line of bare trees,
Farmhouses in the background
Their gray gables rising
Into charcoal clouds.

A solitary figure, slightly bent,
Makes his way
Between the beds,
Moving slowly
Under that heavy sky.

He does not see, cannot know
What aberrant growths
Soon will erupt
Along the cobbled streets
And muddy paths

To occupy the village,
Spread out and line the canals
In their unforgiving phalanxes,
Bringing forth a harvest
Of bones and nameless graves,

The flowers charred, their silky petals
Ground to ash under the iron spikes
Of the juggernauts
Before they too
Finally are swallowed
By the same sodden earth,
The solitary figure
Still walking.

Luciano Pavarotti

He had the sun in his voice,
One critic wrote.
It shone
Through seven decades, spilled over
On the white silk handkerchief
He flourished between arias,
Made luminous
The red tiled roofs of Naples,
Darted in wavelets
Over the Mediterranean,
Spires of Notre Dame, the Tower
And Big Ben,
Glittered
On the sand of Sonora.

But I think
That voice
Was the other woman
In his life, a *prima donna*
Dawn always at her back
Who wrapped herself
Around him, followed
Wherever he went.
She was faithful to the end,
Lying beside him, hearing him
Sing "*Nessun Dorma*" every night
Even when he could no longer speak,
Her arms enfolding
That spent body, holding him
Forever.

Yo-Yo Ma at the Border

Buddha-like,
He plays Bach
In a pocket park
Near the shadow
Of the international bridge.

Sound springs
From his fingers, his bow,
From the strings
And luminous belly
Of his instrument,
A fountain
Dazzling the April green,
A clear stream
Flowing down Laredo's dusty streets
Past the walls and checkpoints,
Past guards and dogs,
The camps and cages

From the park to the river,
From the river
To the sea,
Sweeping us all
Into its breathless, boundless embrace.

Blessing the Animals

for Janice and Bert

We gather in a courtyard
For the ritual. It's muggy today
And the pastor sweats
Beneath his vestments,
Beads already forming
On his brow.
"Bless this cat," he intones.

I remember the stones of Assisi
And its blinding white basilica,
The Saint's damp tomb
His threadbare cloak
Spread like a fan
In its glass case.

Now the pastor
Blesses a goldfish
Darting like a nervous laser
In its paper cup
And touches the scruffy ear
Of a poodle in a tutu.

In the basilica
I'm swallowing Giotto. I see
The luminous hands of St. Francis
Embedded in the fleece of a lamb,
His arms cradling
Its fragile life.

The pastor gives his benediction
To a parrot,
One guinea pig, two snakes
Coiled around the arms
Of a boy,
Another yowling cat.

I think of the Saint again,
Making his vow to Lady Poverty
Before he releases
His flock of doves.

54

Their bright wings scatter the sky,
Sending light
In all directions.

Concert at St. Mark's, San Antonio

for Janice

The 20-something virtuoso
In his white silk jacket
Strides down the center aisle,
Ribbed vaults above him, ornate pews
On either side. Beyond them
Glittering windows
Show the Annunciation,
Moses in the bulrushes.
The soloist reaches the chancel,
Bows to the audience
Takes his seat before the Steinway.

I think of parishioner
Robert E. Lee stepping out
From his stained glass chrysalis
To sit by me,
Carefully positioning his sword
So it won't clatter in the pew.
He's donned his best dress uniform
For the occasion,
Trimmed his beard
Scraped the mud from his boots.

The pianist begins
With an impromptu
But his incandescent hands
Set fire to the keyboard
And he takes us outside
To cool off
In Schubert's rippling brook.
Then we walk
Through Beethoven's moonlit field,
Briefly view the Danube.

If we stay here long enough,
Maybe Lee will sit out Chancellorsville
And miss the road to Gettysburg.

Maybe the bronze Confederate in the park
Will drop his Sharps.
Then the rest of us
Can make our way
Back to the sanctuary
Sifting through the ashes
For slivers of ebony and ivory,
Maybe one lingering spark.

Requiem for a Choirmaster

for Ed and Bert

The shades of his fingers still flit
Over keyboards, pull all the right stops
Of the Aeolian Skinner
That once filled the nave
With thunder and sun.
Pedals still seem to move
At the touch of his feet.

In his prime, he could blow it out.
I almost hear Widor and Bach
Floating toward the vaults, a hundred voices
Belting out "God's Trombones."
They spiral into darkened space,
Curl around stained glass like vines
To seek the life outside.

Hymns settle on the altar
In musty corners
Of the chancel
On the pulpit,
Under pews.
They never will leave,
While a few miles beyond

At his home
He finishes an arrangement
Of "It Is Well with My Soul,"
Leaves his piano
To take his dogs for a walk.
They rise up from their comfortable rug
And follow wherever he goes.

Jazz Mass at San Fernando

The music fuses all in one brief crest
While people file in from the dusty street,
For moments those whose hearts God has possessed.

Fat pigeons settle on the arches, rest,
Wings folded to the tread of weary feet.
The music fuses all in one brief crest.

Long trumpets trail along high columns, dressed
In blues to cross deep rivers, leave the heat,
For moments those whose hearts God has possessed.

Hymns touch the coolness of old stone, sound pressed
Against the silence of stained glass. Lines meet.
The music fuses all in one brief crest

While children breathe the songs and incense, blessed
Fires reaching dark. White candles sing, retreat,
For moments those whose hearts God has possessed.

The priest bows. Oak doors creak toward light, the west
A blaze of singing. Dusk falls like a sheet.
The music fuses all in one brief crest,
For moments those whose hearts God has possessed.

Convent Exhibit

The Sisters canvassed schools
And kindergartens everywhere
For children's art
On themes of peace.

They gathered
Hearts the size of houses
Throbbing in a pond
Or floating through the sky

With swarms of butterflies
Their yellow wings
As big
As palms,

Titanic mothers
Towering in their kitchens,
Windows catching rays
As thick as redwoods

With a rainbow
Battering the door
Below a spray of stars
Impaling trees.

Scattered through these icons
Legends leap in straggly print
Grainy crayon
Dripping tempera

Words like "Love"
And "Home"
"My Favorite Place"
Erupting on butcher paper

Words stretching past the margins,
More insistent, bigger
Even than the ponderous doves,
Their white wings
Pushing through the page.

Children's Chapel, after 9/11

In the loft above, young voices
Float over the organ's thick brass pipes,
Rise like mist
Toward vaults
And stained glass miracles, curling
Around the Savior's spangled head:
"Fairest Lord Jesus..."

In the pews below, teachers
Whisper reprimands to unbowed heads,
Those drumming fingers
And shuffling feet,
But still
The musical crusade
Goes on. Sopranos soar

Beyond the hymn, beyond the walls
To fields of lilies
Blowing somewhere
Past the bombs and black sites
Torture memos and Abu Ghraib
While doves unfold their wings
In perfect unison.

Seeing *Voices in Wartime*

for those in Iraq and Afghanistan

We gather at sundown
In a former church,
Its nave lined with stained glass windows.
Last rays stream
Through their geometric crosses

As the film begins,
Light fading
Until they are opaque,
And all we see is the screen
With its thousands
Of boots on the ground,
Boots on the ground
Light glancing off helmets
And rifles,
Light filling the sky
Over Dresden, bursting
In an apocalyptic cloud
Above Hiroshima,
Soft light
On the grounds of the hospital
Where Sassoon and Owen convalesced
Before they returned
To their deaths,
Light oozing through trenches
And flowing
Down incinerated palms,
Light slanting across the face
Of a grunt who shouts,
"I'm hit!" and then he's gone,
All the light in the world
Shining on piecemeal children,
Their missing limbs.

I pray for darkness,
Unfaltering dark,
The nave so black
I can't see more.
Let it come now.

Rosa's Window, Mission San José

We amble through the grounds
Until we find it
Blackened and baroque,
Stone flowers growing
In their stiff festoons.

And then I think of him,
Huizar
A homesick Spaniard
Carving everything
He'd known

And lost
Into the limestone,
Dust caked in his lashes
Powder
Thickening his palms.

Each day the gray vines
Climbed a few more inches
Underneath his chisel,
Bloomed
Around his hands.

He must have tossed
Through airless nights
Inside the mission
While he dreamed of her
And woke

To face another sweaty morning
In a foreign place.
Then he'd think of home,
Its vaulted spires
And trailing songs

Before he gripped the blade
That could redeem him,
Keep her there
Even as their time
Ran out.

Stranded in a Baltimore Airport

It's midnight, and I've missed my flight.
Another Gulliver, I wander
Through this city of the sleeping,
Would-be passengers slumped over barstools
Or sprawling on benches,
Stretched out on the concourse
While a janitor
Vacuums furiously around them.

I stumble to the children's play space,
Find a downsized train, commandeer
The red caboose.
Inside I curl up, think
Of railroad's glory days:
Iron horses clattering over prairies
Unsettling shaggy herds of buffalo,
Engineers alert for bandits and Apaches.

Then I watch Hollywood's celluloid trains
Come into view and board the Orient Express
To wait for the next strange murder
Before I catch the Silver Streak, grab
A harpoon and try to stay on. Now
I'm the blonde in *North by Northwest*,
All silk and mystery,
Busy saving and seducing Cary Grant.

Hollywood fades to Tokyo
And I ride the bullet train,
Flashing by Mount Fuji
Cherry blossoms a blur
Before I zoom across the Pacific,
Soar over the Golden Gate to land
In Frisco where a clanging cable car
Takes me up the foggy hills.

When I wake,
Coated with dust and dreams
I have morphed into a sudden cosmopolite,

A luscious blonde fluent in Japanese,
A harpoon in one hand
And a Winchester in the other.
No one will know me
When I finally get home.

A Call from New York

Her voice shines on the phone,
Light and iridescent
As soap bubbles
Children blow at the beach.

My daughter's dining on Fifth Avenue,
Gulping down the Guggenheim
Downing great drafts of Times Square
Savoring the library's venerable lions

Thousands of miles
From beeping monitors,
The endless charts and rounds
Her patients moaning in their beds.

She is weightless now
Floating far above biopsies
Flitting like a firefly
Through Picasso, Bach and Stoppard.

I hope she will bring them home
With her, a moveable feast
Stashed under gurneys in the E.R.,
A bite of the Big Apple between surgeries
Maybe a drop of Broadway in someone's IV.

A Court Date in March

I pay my $4.00 parking fee
And enter a maze of beige,
A labyrinth of bleak:
Bare halls, bare walls,
Bare faces in bare rooms.

Clerks direct me
From one blank chamber to the next.
In one of them, a 20-something judge
Looks almost human, asks
What I would like to do.

"What if we splashed a Chagall
Along this corridor,
Piped a sonnet or sestina
Through the PA system, put *Hamlet*
On the video feed?"

Would I then wear my seatbelt?
Would the woman in front of me
Buy insurance? Would her young man
Agree to drive sober,
Stop and render aid?

Once outside, maybe we would notice
Chagall's lovers floating
Along the Interstate or embracing
Underneath a mountain laurel
While Mozart's angels soared
Over the Alamo
And Shakespeare bloomed
On redbuds everywhere.

Inspiration

I read this morning
That Julius Caesar's molecules
Are still around.
We take them in
With every breath,
Inhale his "Et tu, Brute?"
All day long,
His particles of nitrogen
Persisting past fleeting days and dreams.

We might be still closer
To those more recently lost.
Maybe when I jog, huffing my way
Up some unforgiving hill
I'm absorbing
My mother's rich contralto
Or a chord from a Chopin mazurka,
One shade of blue
From a Picasso clown.

Perhaps I even could breathe
The Bard,
Feel his pentameters
Pulsing through my veins,
His sonnets pounding
In my chest
In sudden serendipity,
An accidental tour de force
Another consummation
Devoutly
To be wished.

Crossing Over

A Christmas Eve Conversion

When I was five, my mother took me
To the midnight service. No one
Could weather this much cold.
Coughs rose like incense
From pews and thumped
Against the gothic vaults,
Drowning out the Confession.
Transepts creaked
With random wheezes,
Ice hanging
From our prayers.

I shivered in blue taffeta, squirmed
Through the lessons
Drummed my toes
Against the pew in front.
Mother pushed a Christmas card
Into my hand, a painting
Of a Victorian home,
Green paper garlands
Around a cardboard door,
Lamps on either side
And a fanlight just above.

I left the drafty church,
Its sneezing priest
And stuttered chants, to open
The door. Inside, the necessary fire
Was lit. A nondenominational cat
Dozed by the hearth
While archetypal children
Peered at stockings hung with care.
I walked in to take my place with them,
Soaking up their warmth that night
And after.

Birthday at Glamour Shots

My daughter says they'll fix me up.
I am given choices: sequined jackets,
Turquoise suede, a ruff of ivory lace
Black velvet hats.

A young photographer adjusts my chin,
Tilts my face, croons
"Sit up straight, dear," while I gaze
Into that hungry lens, try
To hold the pose.
"Arch your back and smile..."

Something in his voice, perhaps
The burning light, begins to spin me
Out to other voices, other lights
And I am whirling into time
Floating forward, back again,
My smile lost somewhere in the camera.

I move into the crinkled snapshot
Of a baby's toothless grin,
A laugh caught somewhere in the slats
Of a battered crib
Or I climb mountains
Bursting from the clouds

In southern California,
See flames swaying on a beach
Pacific blue,
Hairpin turns into the Sierras
While I giggle,
Shriek with joy

Inside the school bus
Just before I find
Those other children,
Damp heads heavy on my shoulder
Small hands tugging at my skirt
Larger, larger...

"Hold it...Good!"
We've finished.
I collect the proofs,
Surprised
At all the angles.

A Baja Girlhood

In the Fifties
Our Saturday ritual:
Three miles to Tecate
In a battered jeep,
Hairpin turns on unbanked blacktops,
The occasional cougar
Lounging in an oak,
Sierras encircling us
In their hazy blue parabolas.

At the border the customs inspector
Would wave us through while his wife sang
"La Paloma" in their cottage, her voice
Floating in the thin mountain air.
We would take in stands of eucalyptus,
Dusty streets, brick sidewalks
Lined with children
Selling *chicle*,
Two cafes, a bar, four stores.

The day would unfold
In a sleepy blur. At lunch, the owner
Wouldn't let us pay, walking us
Through his kitchen to show off
His new stove. Then we'd shop:
Silver earrings
And embroidered linens,
Carved boxes pungent
With the scent of mysterious wood.

Finally the brewery: three cases
In the back, a blanket
Casually covering them
So the inspector could save face
And we'd cross over, past the checkpoint
Back to the ranch
And its rattling cattle guards,
Back to long nights of Pacific stars
Mom at her piano.

Small lapses and excesses,
Venial sins. No passports required,
No three-hour waits, body searches
Or drug-sniffing dogs, no heads dangling
From telephone poles or severed hands
Scattered along roadsides,
No *maquiladoras* or mass graves.
Just a junket,
Free lunch and contraband beer.

Baptisms

The beginning:
A priest sprinkles water
On a howling baby's head,
Leaving damp spots
On the ritual white dress
Before the first day of school,
The first kiss, the wedding night
And a first-born child,
First day of spring
And a burst of green leaves,
A first shot in battle
And a call from the hospital,
First funeral
And our first glimpse
Of salt water—
Atlantic, Adriatic, the Sea of Cortez.

Immersion:
St. John dips Jesus
In the Jordan,
Locusts and wild honey
In the background
And we drown
In days, years, decades
Submerged in work and obligation,
Churning through deadlines and schedules
Prayers and protests
Eager for the long hot shower
At the end of a grinding day
And a sudden sinking into sleep
Like the green flash
When the sun drops
Into the Pacific.

Emergence:
We come back to the surface
To receive names that blur
To endings and another start—
A bacillus isolated and labeled,

The disease it causes
Identified, then cured,
An emperor styled "The Great"
Before he shapes a nation, a symphony
Rumbling in someone's brain
Before it rushes onto manuscript
To proclaim itself "Heroic" or "Jupiter,"
A portrait dripping onto canvas
From the artist's palette,
A signature already forming in the corner
As we watch.

Splashtown

Floating in the Wave Pool
For an afternoon,
We all become embryos again,
Swaying
To the pulse
Of its giant, hidden heart.

This vast womb makes us
Family. Sunburned toddlers
Drift by muscled teens, freckled boys
Bump into grandmothers,
Old men glide
By girls in bikinis.

We continue our gestation
On the Lazy River,
Wind our easy way
Between crepes and hibiscus,
Buoyed by breezes
And a honey sun.

But in the end we must be born,
Climbing the steps to spin
Down the spiral slide. Expelled now
To rough water and hot concrete,
We start our exile
With a long walk to the baking car.

Scene in a Parking Lot

"Come back here!"
A father chases his runaway child
As I make my way to Walgreen's.
She tosses her curls, runs faster.
Panting, he catches up, seizes her wrist.
"I don't care
If you don't want to hold my hand.
We're in a parking lot,
And parking lots are dangerous."
She wails.

I think of parking lots
We cross,
Have had to cross
All our lives, often
Without hands to lead
Or stop us
As we move through the maze
Of cars and carts,
That jumble
Of oblivious shoppers,

Hands that cannot reach us
In the office
Or confessional,
The kitchen or bedroom,
The Interstate
Or I-phone,
Hands that cannot help us
When the lab tests come back,
When the twister roars through town
And an IED blows up.

Resigned, she accepts
His determined grip. I reach
The Walgreen's entrance,
And breathe.

Dementia

Where are you today, Dad?
Slogging through mud and bullets
Somewhere in the European Theater?
Training sharpshooters in Puyallup?
Plucking catfish the size of tables
From a pond in the Piney Woods,
Or tuning up the Mercury?
Calibrating a thermostat?

He twitches at his pajamas,
Swats imaginary mosquitoes
From his face,
Kicks his slippers
Across the room.
"Use your sights!" he yells.

An aide brings lunch.
"Your favorite, Sir."
"Stay low," Dad replies.
"Do you want me to cut your carrots?"
"You're aiming too high."
"I'll be back to brush your teeth."
"I'm going on liberty," Dad says,
And closes his eyes.

Rupture

We touch down in Nassau,
Drop into
An envelope
Lined with cream-puff clouds
And coconut palms, flame trees
In bloom by turquoise seas.

Orchids start to grow
On our arms
And white sand
Glitters on our feet
As we drift through tides
And luminous blue waves.

We sip rum to steel drums,
Feast on shrimp, almost glimpse Blackbeard
On an indigo horizon. At dusk
Bob Marley's shade appears. We listen
To his honey voice and feel all right
Until the email

Rips our cocoon, scatters us
To the States, to deadlines
And visitations, long lines of cars.
Exiles from a reformed Pandora's box,
Already we squint into the sun, scan
The skies for signs of cream-puff clouds.

At the Poetry Workshop

for Arch

We have five minutes
To scribble
Examples of frustration
Fast as we can.

Easy. Frustration is the ignition key
Glittering like fool's gold
On the floorboard of my car
After I have pushed the power lock

Or the runs that magically appear
On my last pair of hose,
Lightning striking in the same place
Twice

Or the weekly *jihad* at the store,
Spoils finally taken, my place in line
Secure before I remember
My checkbook on the kitchen table.

Worst of all is the phone
Bleating like an asthmatic goat
Bleating, bleating
A whine that may run out of breath

Before I can seize the handset
And hear your voice,
Curl into its timbre
Like a cat on a favorite rug.

I'm racing for the phone now
Spilling coffee, dropping my pen and paper,
Anything to get there
Put us together

Bring you back
Before the line
Goes
Dead.
"Time," the instructor says.

A Ghazal for Palmer

Another Sisyphus, he rolls that stone uphill.
It falls. He starts again, to meet his unpaid bill.

Some weeks he dodges needles, writes or plays some golf
Until his doctors calculate that unpaid bill.

At first it hid above the jungle green of 'Nam
But then burst orange, cooled into an unpaid bill.

It came home with him to Texas, rolled through stacks, then
Stopped beneath his desk to fatten, the unpaid bill.

For years it grew, bulging underneath his rug
And taking up more space, that mounting unpaid bill.

It followed him into the Thicket, then New York,
Chicago and the South, his faithful unpaid bill,

And even perched on Palo Duro's outcrops, fixed
Before it thudded to new life, still an unpaid bill.

His family, his wife and son, kept vigil, watched
Its spiraling trajectory, that unpaid bill.

One day it came to rest. Then poems and carols bloomed,
Took root, and covered finally the unpaid bill.

In Winter

You don't need a weatherman to know which way the
wind blows—
—Bob Dylan

I feel the cold these days, despite thick coats
And sweaters, woolly socks and scarves I wear
In careful layers while the newsmen blare
Out warnings of black ice, lines down, of boats
Now run aground, of bridges spanning moats
Of snow, while eighteen-wheelers skid and tear
Into the guardrails, jack-knife in the glare
Of cameras. An anchorman devotes
A full ten minutes to the scene. But this
Stale fanfare reinvents calamity,
The fault line underneath our prayers: one match
Misplaced, homes burned, a flood, no SEALs to catch
The terrorists in time, rogue energy
That ripples through our would-be dreams of bliss.

Juvenile

He could be shooting hoops
With neighbors down the street,
One-arm pumps that loop the ball
Through Indian summer days.
Instead he throws a napkin at the wall.

He could be helping in the kitchen,
Heaping cookie dough on trays
In chocolate-studded mounds.
Instead he marches to the big room,
Eats without a fork.

He could be balancing equations,
Finding value in some elegant parabola.
Instead he reckons bricks.
He could be listening to the radio,
Swaying to some heavy beat.

Instead he hears the doors.
They slam electrically into their frames,
Iron meeting iron in perfect sync,
Their weighted edges crashing into place
Cutting off the view
Of anything outside.

Civil Wars

Now Vicksburg's under siege again.   A thick
Smoke hangs in heavy, acrid curls around
Antietam. Oracles appear. They pound
Their fists and often you can hear the click
Of tongues trained on the shattered glass and brick.
Marauders in black cruisers circle, hound
The helpless. Guards have burrowed underground,
While Lincoln dies each day by some new trick.

And it will take more than the searing war
Lee offered up at Appomattox, more
Than shining words at Gettysburg's dark watch
To stop the bloodstained pageant, end the march,
Parade of graves from Ferguson to Watts,
Strides lost to crack and cross-hairs, knives and shots.

White on Black

Somewhere in Florida
A man packing heat
Stands his ground
Against a teen
Armed with Skittles
In the pocket of his hoodie.

In Jasper, another man
Is chained to a truck
And dragged three miles
On a highway
Running through the lush sweet gums
And vines of the Piney Woods.

"I will light you up!"
The cop tells Sandra Bland
At Prairie View
Before he arrests her,
Before she hangs herself
In a Hempstead jail.

In the steam and heat
Of Ferguson
Michael Brown's body
Lies in the sun
On a street
For four hours

And on Staten Island
Eric Garner cries,
"I can't breathe"
Eleven times,
Face down
On the sidewalk.

But in Charlottesville
One skinhead
Hears "La Bamba"
Pouring from someone's boombox
And starts
To dance.

Pledge 2020

On November 3
I will coat
My hands
With sanitizer,
Put on
My heaviest mask
And drive
To the polls.

There I will cast a ballot
For the knee
Lifted from George Floyd's neck,
For a corner diner in Ferguson
Where cops and locals
Sit down
Together
For chilidogs and beer.

I will vote
For lead-free pipes
In Flint,
For skies swept clear
Of greenhouse gas,
For rivers and seas
Flowing beyond
Plastic and sewage.

I will endorse
Refugee children removed
From their cages and returned
To their mothers' arms,
The right of anyone
To see a doctor,
The resurrection
Of truth and fact.

But most of all
On that great day
I will stand and say

Yes to restoration
Of the one institution
Walt Whitman ever praised,
That grand institution
Nearly lost,
"The dear love of comrades."

At Your Service

I pick up the handset
And enter the maze.
"This call may be monitored
For quality assurance,"
An automated voice intones.
I doodle on a legal pad
Count photos on the wall.
"Your call is important to us..."

Metallic music now.
"Thank you for holding..."
I gaze out the window,
Check the polish on my nails.
"Please wait while I connect you..."
Unrecognizable lyrics.
Fingernails start to scratch
Fiber-optic chalkboards

And somewhere in my raw synapses
A thought begins to form.
The idea cools and hardens
In my hand, a new Athena, retooled,
Springing from the brain
Of a disgruntled Zeus,
One blade of iron
Bursting through concrete, growing,

Making its dogged way
Through telephone banks and terminals,
Screens and monitors, miles
Of cable. "Thank you
For your patience,..." Now it's severing
The towers, skewering the satellites.
"Please take the brief survey
At the end of this call..."

While the saw cuts a swath
From Helsinki to Havana,
Bangalore to Boston.

Finally reaching the boardroom,
Its fine teeth spilt
The leather chairs
Of all the stake holders,
Who tumble to the floor, astonished.

"Your call is impor…"
Now they'll have to talk to me.

Vigil for Catherine

We keep it
Late at night
In whispered questions
And uncertain replies
Or at the bank
When we queue up
For a withdrawal.

Sometimes we wait
By her bedroom door
While the florist's truck
Pulls up outside
And the hospice nurse
Hurries back and forth,
A syringe in her hand.

Others far away wait too.
They drum their fingers
On tables and desks,
Text relatives all day
And race for the land line
Pore over emails,
Scan the inbox.

The watch continues
Even in our dreams of other days,
Her high-voltage smile
And laser one-liners,
A rowdy party
Raided by police,
An evening at the symphony.

And when word finally comes,
Our vespers sung, we wait
Some more,
This time trying to believe
Our work is done,
Desperate for some new task
Some untried ritual
To keep our makeshift sacrament
Alive.

Race for the Cure

My daughter wants us all to run
So I grudgingly sign up
And we gather at Sundance Square.
A cruise atmosphere at first, everything
Is pink under a gray sky: pink shirts,
Pink shoes, a 30-foot arch
Of pink balloons.
A rowdy band blares
"Hit Me with Your Best Shot."

Then the starting gun goes off
And 14,000 take the street.
I heave and puff my way up hills
Across an endless flat, around sharp turns.
The elite fly by like urban gazelles,
My daughter and granddaughter waving
As they leave me miles behind.
I shamble along, dream
Of sofas and chocolate eclairs.

But toward the end, we meld
Into sudden, sweaty family: old, young,
Slim, rotund, Latinx, Afro, the woman
In a wheelchair with a baby in her lap, the man
Who jogs with a life-sized poster of his wife.
At last we reach the finish line. Passing
Under a paper rainbow, we collapse
In breathless laughter, almost think
We glimpse a pot of gold.

Elegy for Sandra

She lived in purple, shades that flowered
In the pages of her notebooks,
Scrawled in loopy cursive
Drilled into her fingers by the nuns,
Words curved to orchids
Dangling from a thousand texts.

Purple dripped from her white body,
Left its glowing trail
In polish, perfume, jewels
That glittered in festoons
Along her days,
Shimmered in her nights.

She met the world
Uncompromised
In purple velvet
And a million sequins
Sparkling in the sun,
Glimmering by the moon.

Dazzling life
In wine-dark smiles
And secret odysseys,
Magenta greetings
Stretching
Through her years

She demanded burgundy
And darkest royal blue
For all those pallid mornings
In the hospital, that endless line
Of doctors starched in their white jackets,
Clear glass bottles on a shelf.

The whiter life became,
The more she needed color
Darkening to blood,
Stiffening each night

Thickening her books
Until at last the pages wouldn't turn
And she found angels everywhere
In stores, roads, dusty alcoves, beds
To stay with her
Today, tonight, forever.

A Covid-19 Sacrament

"Wash your hands," the doctors say.
So I wash them.

"Keep calm and wash your hands,"
The Alamodome sign decrees.
Hot water rushes between my fingers
And over my upturned palms.

"Wash your hands long enough to sing
'Happy Birthday to You' twice,"
The radio voice commands.
I work up a rich lather
Foam and bubbles everywhere.
With luck and suds perhaps I'll rid myself
Of every misbegotten molecule,
Each errant cell.

"All the perfumes of Arabia
Will not sweeten this little hand,"
Lady Macbeth laments.
So I wash still more,
Stronger soap and hotter water.
Maybe with such scrubbing I can shed
Those secret silent grudges,
Envy of another's car or dress or poem,
The time I bit my sister's arm
And almost hit a vein,
Her blood dripping on the floor.
I want to rinse it all away,
Rinse off Syria and Yemen,
Iraq and Afghanistan, the toddler's body
Washed up on a Mediterranean shore,
His shoes still neatly tied.

I will strip it all,
Peel off the sickened layers,
Scour through skin, muscle, sinew
Even the memory of Pontius Pilate

Until I finally behold
Clean bones

And wait.

Sleeping Over

Lying in my grandchild's dinosaur day bed,
My toes extending past the footboard
And its jungle comforter,
My head wedged tight
Between two parrots
And a plush giraffe
I listen to the baby's measured breath
Drawing in the sweet air
Of the tropics.

Her room is filled with animals:
A gingham hippo
Floating past a velvet lion
Who stalks imaginary prey for weeks,
A quilted elephant
Who trumpets hours on end,
A zebra night light
White stripes glowing in the dark,
Monkeys jabbering on cotton
While savannahs spread across the carpet
Taking everything
Into their endless reach.

I start to wish
The small shape
Sighing in her unknown dreams
The sinuous speed of cheetahs,
Wits to run past anything
The golden grace of prides
And steamy afternoons
Spent yawning after dinner,
Sense to savor storms
Wasting nothing
In that green expanse
That sweeps across her years.

At the Amusement Park

Everything is slow and gold this afternoon.
My grandchild strolls from ride to ride
The grounds almost deserted.
Leaves trickle from old oaks
In sleepy currents, slow confetti
Floating round our feet in amber swirls.

Painted clowns gaze out from the carousel,
Red smiles peeling
In the thin October light
While they revolve to tinny waltzes,
Horses moving up and down
Their endless hills.

Nearby the Ferris wheel sits unmoving,
Waiting for the children
In their noisy dozens
Who will race in after school
Push and crowd each other to get on,
Shriek as they reach the top.

For now we own the place.
She settles on the roller coaster
Trots toward the waiting cars.
Attendants strap her in, lock the gate,
Pull the lever. The only passenger,
She looks at me serenely

As the train begins its climb
But screams and grips the crossbar
With the first downhill
Louder, harder, with each turn,
Her gold hair blown straight back
In a howl of fear and joy.

I decide that she's too young for this
But now she wants to ride again, at once.
I think about Ulysses.

Visitation

In a darkened car on a muggy night
I keep my grandson company.
Strapped in his booster chair
He waits for his dad to take him
To the airport. Soon the boy will fly,
Alone, across the country.
We talk about the walks we'll take,
The cookies we'll bake, the hoops we'll shoot
Next time.

I put a hand on his armrest and he sees
My swollen veins. His smooth plump fingers
Stroke them thoughtfully
As if they were rivers he could row
To find his long way back.

A Tattoo for My Granddaughter

For her,
Only for her
Would I have this
On my bikini line
To match the one she got last year.
We decided on elephants,
Symbols of remembrance
And long life,
Our history made visible.

The artist scrubs meticulously,
Drenches me
In disinfectant, puts on gloves.
Then he opens the stencils
And it starts:
A steady rain of needles
Tiny punctures
Over and over,
A tactile *Dies Irae*.

I lie still, rub my sweaty palms,
Remind myself that this
Is for the two of us, for twenty years
Of midnight laughter, family feasts
And inexplicable deaths,
Sand-crusted stints at the beach.
Then he's done. A bloody pachyderm
Is born, lumbering across
The broad savannah of my belly.

Now we will trumpet our times together
As we lounge in the shade
Of an acacia, swaying
To the thrum
Of a summer shower,
Rooting around in our thoughts
Bathing luxuriantly
In the river of our memories,
Savoring their warm dust.

And we have the elephants to prove it.

Valediction for Lonesome George

When I read that he had died
I scoured my desk
To find the photo
Slightly yellowed now
Of that day on Santa Cruz.

Leather-limbed
And amiable, his legs
Like mobile tree stumps,
He had lumbered toward me
And sprawled on the sand
Near a *palo santo* tree
While a few frigate birds and tourists
Looked on.

A Galápagos Pinta tortoise
And 90 at the time, he was last
Of his kind, rarest creature on Earth.
His keepers wouldn't let me touch him
But his head shot up
From its weathered carapace
As he gazed at me calmly
Through his wrinkles.

I thought of the decades
He had passed, the weight he had carried
On his gnarled back. Named for a comedian,
He'd outlasted storms
And droughts, whalers and feral goats
Many relocations and failed matings,
Those clutches
That never hatched

But he looked out
At everything
Impervious, beyond extinction
Near the shade of a palo santo tree
Somewhere on Santa Cruz.

A Visit to Merrill, Lynch

For this pilgrimage
I wear my best suit
And highest heels,
Arrive on time
Pass quietly
Through glass doors into the temple,
An apotheosis
In granite, chrome, and steel.

My new priest,
Perfect
In black Armani vestments
Escorts me
To the confessional
Where I enumerate
My lapses
And losses.

He calls me to account
On his computer,
Examines my shortfalls
And shortcomings,
Finally absolves me
But only after exacting a penance
Of fees and dollars,
Aves and promises.

After his blessing
I leave by the sleek elevator
And walk out
Into the emerald afternoon,
Its fallen crepes
And roses
Blooming
Hopelessly.

Watching the Tour de France

Hunched over their handlebars
In high definition, for 21 days
And 2200 miles
Cyclists by the hundreds
Churn up and down
Tree-lined avenues,
Over the Alpe d' Huez
Across the Pyrenees
Their legs driving like pistons
As they pump
Toward some impossible summit,
Sweat rolling down their bodies
In steady streams,
Flames shooting
Through arms, backs, calves
Blood throbbing in their temples
Their muscles like bones,
Their bones hardened
To some new element
We can't name.

They don't seem to notice
The crumbling castles,
Cathedrals with their Gothic spires
Lush vineyards and quaint cobbles,
Seeing only
The colors of the shirts
Ahead of them
And the digital time display.

Watching their taut faces
As they grimly pedal through paradise
I recall my own time in France:
Coffee and croissants
On a terrace in Rouen,
Two days in the Louvre
(Not enough to take in *Winged Victory*),
A night cruise on the Seine.

Back in Texas
I wonder how they can ignore
Those piled-up centuries
Of art and architecture,
Words that set history on fire
Those marble columns on the right
Or the flocks of doves
At Notre Dame.

But I never wore the yellow jersey.

Salute to Cassini

Unlikely paladin
And cosmic knight errant,
You outdid them all
Even Odysseus
On your epic quest,
Your cyber-sword glittering
In all that circuitry.

Like a soldier
On a long and dangerous deployment
For thirteen years
And five billion miles
You skirted planets and moons,
Darting in and out of clouds
And vaporous seas,
Threading your solitary way
Through the heavens,
Around competing atmospheres
Your electric brain telling us
What no one could have guessed,
Your sensors faithfully recording
The unknown and unnamed.
Like Balboa,
You even discovered an ocean.

And when you could journey no more,
You hurtled into rest
Somewhere within Saturn's rings,
A briefly brilliant offering
For all
Who ever looked up,
And marveled.

On the Summit of Aspen Mountain

At 10,000 feet,
Far above
The pretty city
With its sleek boutiques
And glossy galleries,
Those manicured lawns
And perfectly groomed poodles,
Everything ascends:

Light rises
In the stands of spruce and fir,
Green sweeping up
Through their branches,
A trumpet's solitary soaring melody
Rebounding off peaks
And outcrops,
Spiraling up
Into a radiant sky.
Even the scree and stubble
Seem to float
While the wind
Lifts in a constant hymn,
Almost a prayer.

In Oklahoma

They are here,
In the depths of red earth
Between the blades
Of buffalo grass—
Chickasaw, Cherokee, and Osage.

They breathe
In the green veins
Of hickory leaves, in the needles
Of wind-bent pines—
Chickasaw, Chocktaw and Pontotoc.

They sleep
To the song
Of an apricot
Shaman moon—
Chocktaw, Washita, Caddo and Atoka.

They wait behind
The pump jacks,
Above the hoods
Of rusty pickups—
Cherokee, Comanche and Osage.

They watch
By the walls of the tricksters,
By their neon green
Money machines—
Tishomingo, Pontotoc and Osage.

They give their names, their blood
To turnpikes, bridges
Streets
And towns—
Chickasaw, Shawnee, and Broken Bow.

They fly under the wings
Of the scissortail,
Float in clouds

Scudding across a cinnabar sky—
Chickasaw, Chocktaw, Cherokee,
Shawnee, Osage, Comanche,
Pontotoc and Tishomingo,
Comanche and Atoka.
They are here.

Northern Palace, Palenque

Ambling through its tiny rooms, I ponder
This apotheosis in crumbling stone, flaking ceilings
Inches over my head. Feeling only heat and sweat,
I notice vacantly a ceiba shoot
Bursting through a wall, its leaves
Fat and insistent,
Green as a new thought.

Suddenly I see those who waited for rain here,
Had their meals, made love
And brought forth children, filled the space
With fleeting song. Their scent now on my skin,
I leave behind my camera and bottled water
To enter their blood,
Their bones.

Restoration

I have taken on my patio wilderness,
Savage after ten years of neglect.
English ivy tangles power lines
And curls across windows
In an impromptu parade.
Japanese yews shoot
Above the roofline, split shingles,
While hackberries
Heavy with wasps' nests
Spew their furious red fruit.

A Millennial Eve,
I want to saw my way back to Eden
But the way is hard.
Sweat drips from my hair, face, shirt
In salty rivulets, spatters
On hot cement. Digging out crab grass
Sows a bumper crop
Of blisters on my palms
And I remember Adam's curse.

Still, somehow
After many angry days
I start to see
Rough outlines of another place:
No archangel
With a flaming sword,
No fateful prophecies
Just a possibility of green
Glowing on fresh-cut branches.

Breaking the Stump

for Gene

He started at first light,
Slicing through the ruin
Of a Texas oak with handsaw and ax.
All morning he cut and dug,
Cut and dug
While sweat poured down him
In a steady stream, matted his hair,
Turned his shirt
From blue to black.

Sometimes he would mutter in Portuguese,
Mop his brow or straighten his back
But he never stopped,
While noon turned to evening
And light began to fade
In the flying dust.
By nightfall nothing was left
But empty earth. He put his tools away,
Finally pulled off his boots.

This morning I planted a new tree
In the space he had made.
Today an assortment of twigs,
This Brazilian rattlebox soon
Will dapple the blazing patio with green
And bloom in the language
Of his forebears, sending out a thousand
Orange melodies for all to hear.
Every leaf will sing his name.

Legacy

I found her nest
In an overgrown ligustrum.
A waxwing, or maybe a cardinal,
She'd left a tightly-woven miscellany
Of twigs and newsprint,
Thread and Styrofoam
A makeshift artifact
Still wedged
Between two branches
Long after her brood had flown.

I imagine her skimming the headlines
Before she left each morning
To grub out her living,
Daily events woven into her
The way, today, I glance at the early edition
In my kitchen
Before I thread my way
Through traffic and a tangled schedule
Trying to build
Something that endures.

Heirloom

This small room
Cramps our old four-poster.
Its finials, perfect tears
That someone turned
A hundred years ago,
Graze the sheetrock ceiling.

Red walnut vines
Trail along the headboard,
Spiraling in stiff festoons
Toward another place, long gone,
Where all the doors had transoms
And the bedrooms opened
On a balcony
Where anyone could hear
The mourning doves
Or look for the Big Dipper.
The stars often were lost in coastal fog
But when the night was clear
We'd carry them to bed
Where they would warm us,
Lighting up the leaves and tendrils
Curling through the wood.

Today I run my hand
Along the grain,
My fingers
Searching out
The shapes
Of all those buried stars.

Mother Arm

for Ruth

My daughter drives, our seatbelts clicked in place,
To see a show downtown and I replay
Her early years, no car seat for a brace

When I would swing my arm around her, pray
That was enough, each time I had to stop
Or turn. "That mother arm," she used to say.

We drain our Pepsis to the final drop
And watch *The Butler*, see him move through change:
Oil embargoes, Watergate and Woodstock,

Three decades, seven presidents, a range
Of crises. Credits roll and then the light
Goes off. Lost in the dark, caught in the strange

Transition out of history, I fight
For footing on the stairs and stumble, feel
At once my daughter's touch, her warm hand tight

Around my arm to guide me as we deal
With crowds who hunger for a 3-D thrill
Served up with buttered popcorn. In their zeal

They push and jostle us, a giddy mill
Of teens intent on viewing scripted harm,
Plastique and painless love, the easy kill.

At last we reach the doors and leave the swarm
To breathe blue night, its sweep of fleeting clouds
And silent stars, her hand still on my arm.

Reprise

Redoing a guest room, I take down
His painting of the park done decades ago,
Still luminous like old porcelain, like water
In clear glass. Arthritic now, on Lipitor, I gaze
At those broad brush strokes, those sweeps
Of ochre, green and gold and almost feel
Damp grass beneath my back,
A flutter of leaves in my hair.

I think of those long nights
When we were new-made forest gods,
When I would slip out after curfew
To meet him there
And we would walk
Those gravel paths, sit back to back
Under an oak to name the constellations,
Count the drifting stars.

On the back of the canvas I find
His inscription under a filigree heart,
Cupid's inevitable arrow
Cutting through the center in black ink,
A faded flourish on the last letter
Of my name still blurred
Into the first letter of his,
Still clear after all these years.

Signing the Will

I scrawl my name and the date
On page after page, form after form,
Raise my right hand
And swear that I have been truthful.
The notary affixes her stamp
And I dispose of my earthly goods.

But with that vow
I silently make another:
I wish my children
Noisy family feasts
Rowdy toasts
And lemon pie

Or time in Tanzania watching elephants
Lumber across the savannah,
Trumpeting to the heavens
And kicking up
Majestic clouds of dust,
Kilimanjaro in the background

Or miles of Mozart along a tranquil beach,
The copper sun sizzling as it drops
Into the Gulf, along with leagues of Bach,
His *Brandenburg Concertos* blowing
Through conch shells,
Leaving perfect sand dollars in their wake.

I wish them too the alchemy of others:
A touchstone in the private joke
That still draws laughs,
A knowing hand
That reaches past sinew, muscle, bone
To find the vein of gold.

But most of all, I wish my kin
Journeys that burst with light,
Blind them
In the end
Like Saul
On the road to Damascus.

Pearl

for Adam and Ruta

I dreamed you
And you were there,
Before your parents
First drew breath,
Before they toddled off
To kinder, then to college,
Walked the stage
And fell into each other's lives.
I dreamed you

And you were there
At their wedding,
Before they made their vows
And the band played
"When the Saints Go Marching In,"
Before the marriage feast, before
They danced
And cut their cake
I dreamed you

And you were there
Before you quickened,
Turning cartwheels
In your mother's womb,
Before your inch-long arms
Stretched out to touch
Her veins, her dark, pulsing walls
Before you kicked her
Into morning.

And when at last
You came to us,
Each digit pink and perfect,
Your cry a high-pitched hymn
I woke, my long dream
Vanishing
In your greater light.

50th High School Reunion, East Texas

For two days I dip into youth:
The first self-conscious prom,
My corsage pinned awkwardly
And falling off my formal,
Rowdy football games
The first kiss
In Grandmother's Victorian parlor,
The first illicit drink.

For that time I don't see
The present: my former flame
With a beer belly, our best cheerleader
In a walker, the homecoming queen
Who can't hear,
The sweet-armed quarterback
Gliding across the dance floor
In his wheelchair.

But outside, the land spreads before me
Like pages of an endless book:
Mourning doves croon along the margins,
Oil rigs hiss and thrum between the fence lines
Like an army of giant hearts
While Herefords, Beefmasters, Brahmas
Amble across the text,
Slow-moving sculptures huddling under oaks
Even in August,
All facing the same way
Their large eyes fixed on some luminous point
Hidden in the Spanish moss.

www.ingramcontent.com/pod-product-compliance
Lightning Source LLC
Chambersburg PA
CBHW020803020726
47495CB00008B/2567